The Foundations Book

The Foundations Book

Portions of this content were taken and modified from *The Way To Win* by Jeff Little.

www.milestonechurch.com

ISBN: 978-1-954961-08-1
Printed in the United States.

THE CHAPTERS

HERE'S WHY WE DEVELOPED THIS RESOURCE

1. FOLLOWERS OF JESUS OBEY HIM.

- In Matthew 7:24, Jesus said the wise person builds their life not just by hearing His words, but actually putting them into practice.
- Culture says: "Live your truth. Follow your heart." Jesus says, "Follow me."

2. FOLLOWERS OF JESUS READ AND STUDY THE BIBLE.

- The Bible can be intimidating but the best way to learn is to have someone help you.
- In each chapter of this book, you have multiple opportunities to read and write down passages of Scripture for yourself.

3. FOLLOWERS OF JESUS REALIZE IT'S LESS ABOUT WHAT YOU KNOW AND MORE ABOUT WHO YOU ARE BECOMING.

- You will find several opportunities to apply and live out the concepts you are learning in practical ways.
- We do not do spiritual things in order to earn God's love. But when you understand how much God loves you, you want to live in a way that honors and pleases Him.

4. FOLLOWERS OF JESUS LEARN AND SHARE WITH OTHERS.

- It has often been said that the best way to learn something yourself is to teach it to someone else.

Hopefully, this will not be a book you flip through once and then set on a shelf. We designed it to meet an important need. As a pastor who has worked closely with people from all different backgrounds for more than three decades, I believe people want to grow in their relationship with God . . . but they don't know how.

This resource was designed to help fill that gap. My prayer is that God will use it to initiate meaningful and dynamic conversations with family members, friends, co-workers, and the people you care about most.

You can go through the book yourself, with another person, or in a small group. Once you're finished, I believe you will discover its value and gain the confidence to invite someone else to experience it too.

I am so excited for you to go on this journey, and I'm trusting God will use it to draw you closer to Him and to every person who joins you along the way.

JEFF LITTLE

THE LAYOUT

EACH CHAPTER FOLLOWS A PATTERN:

- The important, fundamental question
- Bible verses to look up and write down
- The concept
- The passage
- Application to your everyday life
- Reflection and discussion questions

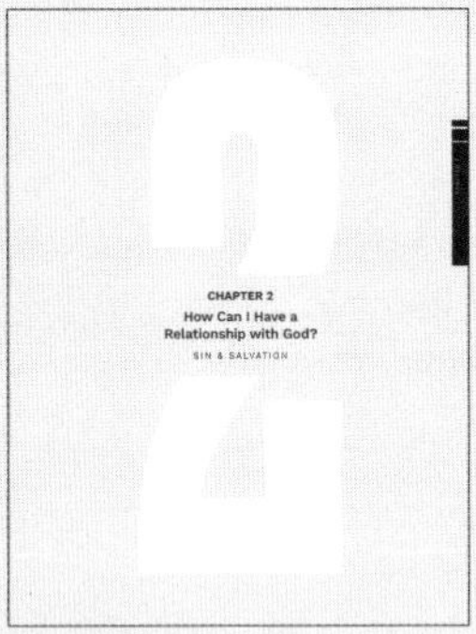

FUNDAMENTAL QUESTION

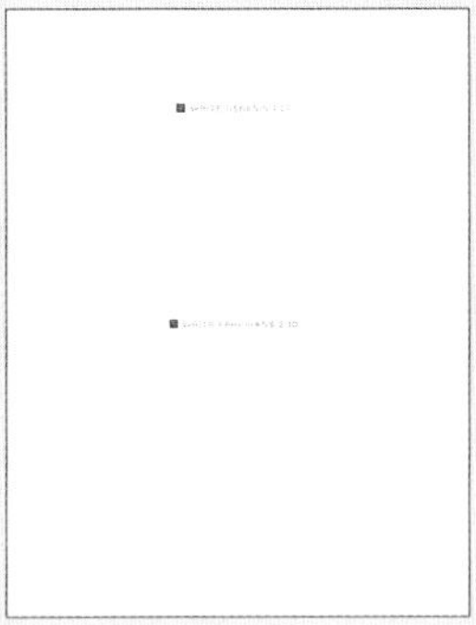

BIBLE VERSES

THE CONCEPT

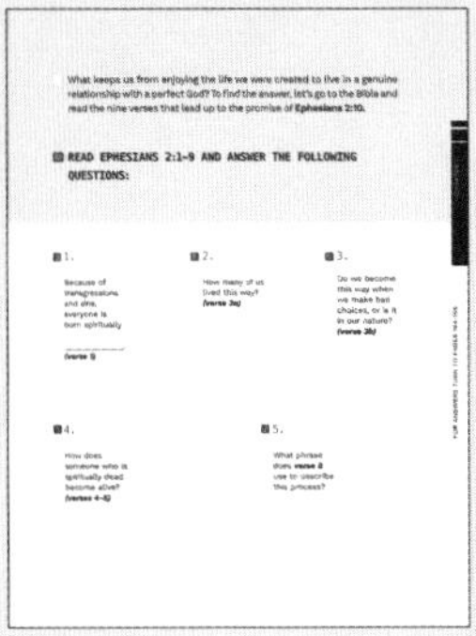

THE PASSAGE

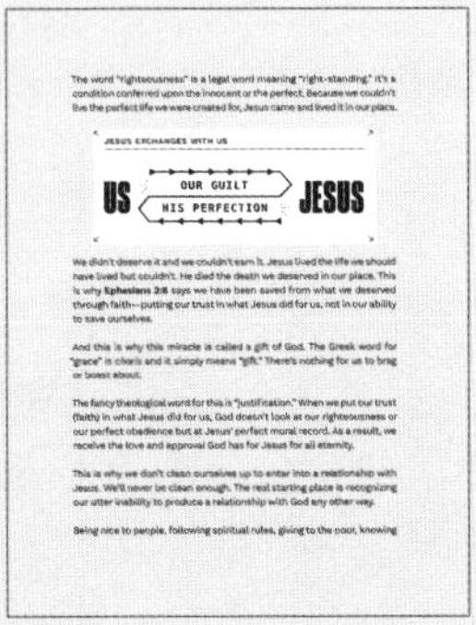

APPLICATION

REFLECTION AND DISCUSSION QUESTIONS

THE PLAN

Write down thoughts or questions as you're reading!

READ AND INTERACT WITH THE CONCEPTS.

You'll get the most out of this journey if you look up the verses in your Bible, answer the questions, underline key concepts, and write down thoughts or questions as you're reading.

TALK ABOUT IT.

This book is designed for relationships more than individual study. From the beginning, followers of Jesus have gathered with another person or in small groups to study and consider His message.

PASS IT ON.

Once you finish this book, the best way to grow deeper in your understanding is to take someone else through the process you just completed.

CHAPTER

1 WHAT AM I BUILDING MY LIFE ON?

2 HOW CAN I HAVE A RELATIONSHIP WITH GOD?

3 HOW DO I CHANGE AND BEGIN MY NEW LIFE IN CHRIST?

4 WHAT DOES GOD WANT FROM ME?

5 HOW DO I HEAR FROM GOD?

6 HOW CAN I EXPERIENCE GOD'S PRESENCE EVERY DAY?

7 WHERE HAS GOD PLACED ME?

8 HOW DOES GOD THINK ABOUT MONEY?

9 WHY IS THE CHURCH IMPORTANT?

10 WHAT DO I DO NOW?

1

CHAPTER 1

What Am I Building My Life On?

INTRODUCTION & OVERVIEW

WRITE JOHN 17:3.

WRITE 1 CORINTHIANS 3:11.

We only get one chance at life. So we want to make the most of it. We want to experience the absolute best that life has to offer.

In our world, we have more options and more information about what everyone else is doing than any previous generation. It's no wonder we're all a little anxious and worried about missing out.

Have you ever considered,

"WHAT AM I BUILDING MY LIFE ON?"

THIS IS A FOUNDATIONAL QUESTION.

We need a plan, a guide that helps us understand what really matters so we can make the right choices. Without a plan, we are left to live from choice to choice, hoping things work out. Unfortunately, this is where too many of us end up. Twenty-five-hundred years ago, the philosopher Socrates famously said, "The unexamined life is not worth living."

We all build on something—and the foundation you choose determines the life you live.

WHAT IF THERE WAS A PURPOSE FOR YOUR LIFE BEFORE YOU WERE BORN?

WHAT IF GOD HIMSELF HAD A PLAN UNIQUELY DESIGNED JUST FOR YOU?

WOULD YOU WANT TO KNOW WHAT IT WAS?

WOULD YOU ASK FOR HELP TO DISCOVER IT?

In **John 17**, Jesus is moments away from being arrested. In less than 24 hours, He'll be beaten and die the most excruciating death imaginable on a cross along a busy road. Before this happens, Jesus prays and asks God for help. In this prayer, He gives us an insight into what really matters in life.

When Jesus says in **John 17:3**, "Now, this is eternal life..." He is speaking about more than the quantity of life—a life that never ends. He's talking about the quality of life—the life we were created to live.

The life we were all created to live is built on the foundation of knowing God and Jesus Christ, the One God sent to be with us. This is the life that is truly life. Jesus came to make this abundant life available to any of us who would receive Him.

This is more than knowing information about Him. It means to know and be known, to walk with Him, to trust Him when we don't understand, and to see the reality of His presence in every area of our lives.

A man named Paul experienced this firsthand. He went from persecuting those who followed Jesus to developing a genuine, personal relationship with Him. And God used him to help establish the early church. Through great opposition, danger, and supernatural outcomes, Paul planted churches, trained leaders, and preached the message of Jesus throughout the Roman Empire. His letters to churches make up a large percentage of the New Testament.

In his first letter to the church located in the first-century city of Corinth, Paul is frustrated because the people are being foolish. They're fighting with each other over foolish personal preferences. They're building on a foolish plan. They have the wrong foundation.

Paul says that it was by God's grace that he laid a foundation like a skilled master builder. In **1 Corinthians 3:11**, Paul tells us that there's only one foundation for a wise person to build on: Jesus Christ.

THE LIFE WE WERE ALL CREATED TO LIVE IS BUILT ON THE FOUNDATION OF KNOWING GOD AND JESUS CHRIST.

THAT IS THE SIMPLE PURPOSE OF THIS BOOK.

WHAT DOES IT MEAN TO BUILD YOUR LIFE ON JESUS?

HOW DOES THAT WORK?

WHAT HAPPENS WHEN WE BUILD THIS WAY?

This was not a theory for the disciples, for Paul, or for the earliest followers of Jesus. They were not following spiritual traditions or the moral obligations of a religious belief system. They built their lives on a personal relationship with Jesus. And not only did it change them, but it also changed their families, their neighborhoods, their cities, and eventually the whole world.

The mission of God, His Kingdom, and His Church are all advancing through the earth today because of the foundation of Jesus Christ. And He offers this same hope to you and me today.

THE MISSION OF GOD, HIS KINGDOM, AND **HIS CHURCH ARE ALL ADVANCING THROUGH THE EARTH TODAY BECAUSE OF THE FOUNDATION OF JESUS CHRIST.**

READ MATTHEW 7:24–29 AND ANSWER THE FOLLOWING QUESTIONS:

! Questions and Answers throughout this book are based on the NIV translation of the Bible. If you are reading a different version of the Bible, simply write your answers based on your reading.

1.

In ***verse 24***, Jesus says, "Everyone who hears these words of mine and puts them into practice . . . " What's the difference between "hearing" and "putting into practice"?

2.

What happens to the house in ***verse 25***? Why?

3.

What metaphor does Jesus use to describe someone who hears His words but doesn't do them? ***(verse 26)***

4.

What happens to the foolish builder's house? ***(verse 27)***

FOR ANSWERS TURN TO PAGES 154-155

5.

How did the crowds respond to Jesus' teaching? Why did they react this way? ***(verses 28-29)***

Jesus' teaching on the wise and foolish builders is among His most well-known. Maybe you've heard it before. But when you think about it, it's bold. It's aggressive. It's a long way from "Follow your heart" or "Do what makes you happy."

Consider for a moment the basic premise. The question is not, "Will we face rain, floods, or winds?" Whatever words we choose to use, the meaning remains the same. Every single person will face challenging circumstances. You could say all of us are in one of three places at any given time in our lives: **(1)** in a storm, **(2)** coming out of a storm, or **(3)** headed for a storm.

The question is, "**What foundation are you building on?**" Because ultimately, building your own kingdom can't hold up to the floods and challenges of life, and it will leave you insecure, anxious, and hopeless in your own strength.

Anytime people in the ancient world thought about buildings and foundations, they thought about the concept of a "cornerstone." In architecture, particularly with stone, the cornerstone is the most vital piece of the foundation. Not only does it fasten and secure the foundation, but it sets the alignment of the entire structure.

CORNERSTONE

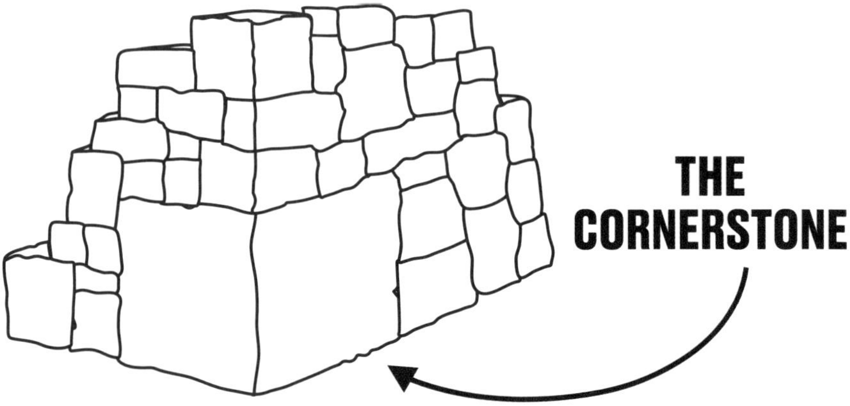

Every other stone fits into its place based on its relationship with the cornerstone. Until it's secure, nothing else can be built. **Psalm 118** is a song about God's goodness and how He offers salvation, and in verse 22 it says, "The stone the builders rejected has become the cornerstone." It's a prophetic picture of how God offers Jesus as the foundation. In **Isaiah 28:16**, God says He lays a precious cornerstone and the one who relies on it will never panic.

God wants you to build your life on Jesus. He has a plan for everything you care about in life. But without Jesus as the cornerstone, when the storms come, everything will come crashing down.

How are you building? Whether we acknowledge it or not, we all have a cornerstone. It could be your career, family, finances, or yourself and your own plans. While these things are good, and God has a purpose for them all, they ultimately can be shaken and washed away—that's what Jesus is telling us in **Matthew 7**.

WE NEED SOMETHING ETERNAL TO PLACE OUR TRUST IN AND BUILD OUR LIVES UPON.

We need something eternal to place our trust in and build our lives upon. Jesus offers Himself as the chief cornerstone of our lives. The question is, "Will you not only hear Jesus' words, but will you also *do* them?"

Remember, it's not about what you know or don't know. Jesus is after your heart. Will you trust Him? Will you say yes and keep taking steps to follow Him?

You can do it and this journey is designed to help you get there.

REFLECT//DISCUSS

1. WHAT DO YOU THINK IT MEANS TO BUILD YOUR LIFE ON JESUS?

2. AFTER READING THIS CHAPTER, WHAT WOULD YOU SAY YOU'VE BEEN BUILDING YOUR LIFE ON UP TO THIS POINT? HOW IS THAT DIFFERENT FROM BUILDING YOUR LIFE ON JESUS?

3. DO YOU TRUST JESUS WITH EVERY AREA OF YOUR LIFE? ARE THERE ANY AREAS WHERE YOU ARE HOLDING BACK? EXPLAIN.

4. AS YOU START GOING THROUGH *THE FOUNDATIONS BOOK*, WHAT DO YOU HOPE TO GET OUT OF IT?

CHAPTER

1 WHAT AM I BUILDING MY LIFE ON?

2 HOW CAN I HAVE A RELATIONSHIP WITH GOD?

3 HOW DO I CHANGE AND BEGIN MY NEW LIFE IN CHRIST?

4 WHAT DOES GOD WANT FROM ME?

5 HOW DO I HEAR FROM GOD?

6 HOW CAN I EXPERIENCE GOD'S PRESENCE EVERY DAY?

7 WHERE HAS GOD PLACED ME?

8 HOW DOES GOD THINK ABOUT MONEY?

9 WHY IS THE CHURCH IMPORTANT?

10 WHAT DO I DO NOW?

CHAPTER 2

How Can I Have a Relationship with God?

SIN & SALVATION

WRITE GENESIS 1:27.

WRITE EPHESIANS 2:10.

You are not an accident.
You are more than a collection of atoms. Your life is significant and filled with deep meaning. There is a purpose for your life.

YOU WERE MADE TO BE WITH GOD.

THINK ABOUT THAT.

THE

INFINITE,

ETERNAL,

UNCREATED

GOD

NOT ONLY KNOWS

YOUR NAME,

EVERY DETAIL

OF YOUR LIFE,

AND

ALL YOUR **DEEPEST**

FEARS AND HOPES,

BUT HE ALSO **WANTS** TO

HAVE **A RELATIONSHIP**

WITH ***YOU.***

This message is clear throughout all of Scripture. We were created in the image of God—to look like Him and to add our part in reflecting His goodness to the rest of the world.

This word "handiwork" from Ephesians 2:10 is meant to evoke the product of a master craftsman who skillfully and intentionally develops each piece. Another version chooses the word "masterpiece." But you're not meant to sit on a shelf or hang in a museum.

YOU HAVE GIFTS AND ABILITIES ENTRUSTED TO YOU TO BE SHARED FOR THE BENEFIT OF OTHERS.

For your service, you experience fulfillment and joy, and God receives glory. It's this incredible, life-giving cycle that adds value to everyone.

This may sound naïve and idealistic, but it's what the Bible says. You were created in God's image to enjoy with Him everything He made, as you use your gifts to steward all you've been given.

YOU HAVE GIFTS AND ABILITIES ENTRUSTED TO YOU TO BE SHARED FOR THE BENEFIT OF OTHERS.

If you've ever wanted to use your gifts in meaningful work for something bigger than yourself, this is the reason. It's why people often say they're inspired watching an artist or a craftsman use their talents. We were created to live this way.

While we sometimes experience glimpses of this reality, these moments are rare and fleeting. Regular, everyday life has all kinds of problems. We can't get it how we want it, and even when we do, it doesn't deliver like we expect. And most of the time, we're not sure how God fits into what we're doing. We feel separate and distant from Him.

What keeps us from enjoying the life we were created to live in a genuine relationship with a perfect God? To find the answer, let's go to the Bible and read the nine verses that lead up to the promise of **Ephesians 2:10.**

READ EPHESIANS 2:1–9 AND ANSWER THE FOLLOWING QUESTIONS:

1.

Because of transgressions and sins, everyone is born spiritually

________________.

(verse 1)

2.

How many of us lived this way? ***(verse 3a)***

3.

Do we become this way when we make bad choices, or is it in our nature? ***(verse 3b)***

4.

How does someone who is spiritually dead become alive? ***(verses 4–5)***

5.

What phrase does ***verse 8*** use to describe this process?

FOR ANSWERS TURN TO PAGES 154-155

The reason you can't live the life you were created to live is because you can't live a perfect life with a perfect God if you're not perfect.

Even the best among us realize we're not perfect. We make mistakes. We hurt others with our words and choices—often the people we love the most. And the problem in this passage goes deeper than what we do or say—it even extends to what we want and what we think.

You see, the thing about a perfect God is, He knows us so completely that He sees past our facade to what's really going on inside us.

We don't need help feeling guilty. We feel guilty because we are guilty. We know we come up short. The world is a broken place; real evil exists out there. But the deeper problem isn't the evil that's "out there"—it's the capacity for evil on the inside of us that's truly terrifying.

This tendency, which can be found in exactly every human being who has ever lived, is called sin. Not only do we make mistakes we come to regret, but we often know what the right choice is and instead choose the thing we know is wrong because it's what we want.

Most of us give ourselves too much credit. This is fundamental to the human condition. Psychologists call this *self-serving bias*. We all have the tendency to take credit for any success around us while we blame others for our mistakes. As a culture, we cling to the idea that we're all basically good, but we wouldn't like the results if someone followed us and kept score of every sinful deed, thought, and desire we had—even for one day.

THIS TENDENCY,
WHICH CAN BE FOUND IN
EXACTLY **EVERY HUMAN BEING**
WHO HAS EVER LIVED,
IS CALLED **SIN.**

↓

SO WHAT ARE OUR OPTIONS
TO DEAL WITH THE PROBLEM OF

SIN?

↓

1. TRY REALLY HARD TO BE PERFECT.

It doesn't work. It's exhausting. And it's the fastest way to become aware of how messed up everyone else is because they're not trying as hard as you are to do the right thing. Trying to be perfect is a guaranteed approach to make your life miserable.

2. DECIDE THAT BECAUSE WE'RE NOT PERFECT, GOD'S NOT PERFECT EITHER.

The problem with this option is that we end up with a god who looks like us. This gives a great boost to our pride but the value wears off really quickly. A god like us doesn't have much to offer.

3. FIND SOMEONE WHO IS PERFECT TO BE A SUBSTITUTE ON OUR BEHALF.

If you've been to the airport in recent years, you've likely experienced waiting in a long security line. You wait your turn to be examined in order to gain admittance to the other side by stepping into the big gray machine that spins and takes your picture.

The security people tell everyone to take out their laptops, take off their shoes—you know the song-and-dance routine. If you travel semi-regularly and pay even moderate attention, you understand there are some things they'll never let through.

Imagine if one of those non-negotiable items wasn't packed in your carry-on—it was in your heart. You can't take it off like shoes, a belt, or a watch. You can't throw it out like a knife or a bottle containing more than 3.5 fluid ounces.

It's part of you.

In that situation, the only chance you have to get to the other side is if someone else gets in the scanner for you.

This is precisely what Ephesians 2 is describing. This is what Jesus did on the cross.

Because God is perfect, He can't allow evil and injustice to continue without being dealt with.

THIS LEAVES TWO OPTIONS:

1. We have eternal separation from God.

2. We are made righteous
and alive to be with God forever.

In 2 Corinthians 5:21, Paul writes about Jesus this way: **"God made him who had no sin to be sin for us, so that in him we might become the righteousness of God."**

1. According to this verse, what did Jesus not have?

2. Who did Jesus become sin for?

3. The words "so that" tell us why. Why did God make Jesus to be sin for us?

FOR ANSWERS TURN TO PAGES 154-155

The word "righteousness" is a legal word meaning "right-standing." It's a condition conferred upon the innocent or the perfect. Because we couldn't live the perfect life we were created for, Jesus came and lived it in our place.

We didn't deserve it and we couldn't earn it. Jesus lived the life we should have lived but couldn't. He died the death we deserved in our place. This is why **Ephesians 2:8** says we have been saved from what we deserved through faith—putting our trust in what Jesus did for us, not in our ability to save ourselves.

And this is why this miracle is called a gift of God. The Greek word for "grace" is *charis* and it simply means "gift." There's nothing for us to brag or boast about.

The fancy theological word for this is "justification." When we put our trust (faith) in what Jesus did for us, God doesn't look at our righteousness or our perfect obedience but at Jesus' perfect moral record. As a result, we receive the love and approval God has for Jesus for all eternity.

This is why we don't clean ourselves up to enter into a relationship with Jesus. We'll never be clean enough. The real starting place is recognizing our utter inability to produce a relationship with God any other way.

Being nice to people, following spiritual rules, giving to the poor, knowing lots of facts about the Bible—these things have value and may improve the quality of our lives, but they don't have the power to save us.

Only trusting in the perfect obedience and love of Jesus can do that. Because of this, we receive access to God's original plan—to live the life we were created to live.

The truth is, this isn't easy.

First, many of us have to overcome barriers in our minds. The pain of poor choices can lead you to believe you're beyond hope. Or you feel like because of what someone else did to you, you'll never be able to completely put those painful experiences behind you.

Jesus spoke to people in both of these groups—and He helped them overcome these challenges.

Next, it's not easy to be honest and humble enough to admit your need for a Savior. But on the other side of this willingness, you'll discover a power far beyond your own ability.

Finally, there's often a hesitation from this simple thought: *Can I live up to this?* It sounds so compelling, so exciting, which only increases the pressure. No one wants to fail. No one wants to be a hypocrite. But when you understand that your ability to live this way is not a function of your willpower, you're free to step into this new life in Christ.

REFLECT// DISCUSS

1. HOW DOES THIS DESCRIPTION OF WHAT IT MEANS TO HAVE A RELATIONSHIP WITH GOD DIFFER FROM WHAT YOU PREVIOUSLY THOUGHT?

2. DO YOU HAVE ANY HESITATION OR RELUCTANCE TO TAKE THIS NEW STEP BECAUSE OF HOW YOU WERE RAISED? ARE YOU WORRIED ABOUT HOW YOU WOULD EXPLAIN THIS TO YOUR FAMILY?

3. DO YOU HAVE THIS KIND OF A RELATIONSHIP WITH GOD? WOULD YOU LIKE TO? WHAT'S HOLDING YOU BACK?

4. HAVE YOU EVER THOUGHT ABOUT YOUR NEED FOR A SAVIOR? EXPLAIN.

5. DO YOU EVER WORRY THAT YOU CAN'T LIVE THE LIFE GOD HAS FOR YOU? IF SO, WHAT ARE YOUR FEARS OR CONCERNS?

If you've never prayed to make Jesus your Savior and Lord, you can do it right now. Just read these words out loud, and say them from your heart:

Jesus,
I am a sinner in
need of a Savior.
I believe You are God.
I believe You died
on the cross for my sins.
I ask You to forgive
me and to save me.
Would You please take
my guilt and give me
Your perfection?
Thank You for saving me.
In Jesus' name I pray.
Amen.

If you just prayed that prayer for the first time, your next step is to tell someone. Don't keep it to yourself! If you're going through this book with a small group or with a friend, tell them. They will be excited to know. Then keep going through this book every week to learn more about God and how to grow in your relationship with Him.

CHAPTER

CHAPTER 3

How Do I Change and Begin My New Life in Christ?

REPENTANCE & BAPTISM

WRITE 2 CORINTHIANS 7:10.

WRITE ACTS 26:20.

Change is a constant in life, but it's not easy. We spend a lot of time and energy trying to figure it out. You're reading this book because you want to grow and change.

It can be fun to think about change. It's more difficult to actually do it.

We like the benefits of change more than we like the process. All change begins with the painful realization of where you really are—not where you'd like to be, not your idealized sense of self, not a slightly lesser version of someone you admire.

You have to see the real you. You have to confront the brutal facts. As painful as this can be, it's a gift because it reveals your need to change.

Once you get the brutal facts, you have two options:

(1) receive it and change, or (2) resist and stay trapped.

- If you want to get in shape, you don't get mad at your trainer at the gym.
- If you want to grow in professional skills, you don't argue with your coaching assessment.
- If you want to be a better friend, you don't attack them when they give you honest feedback.

This is what **2 Corinthians 7:10** describes as the difference between worldly sorrow and godly sorrow. Worldly sorrow is feeling sorry for yourself because you were challenged or critiqued. You don't feel bad for what you did—you feel bad because you were called on it.

Worldly sorrow has no power to change you. Instead, the self-pity typically drives you right back into the poor choices you made in the first place.

FOR ANSWERS TURN TO PAGES 154-155

According to 2 Corinthians 7:10, what does worldly sorrow bring?

Godly sorrow is a whole different ballgame. You see yourself from a right perspective and you're willing to do whatever it takes to change. People who are willing to learn, even when it's painful, end up changing and growing. The Bible calls this "repentance."

It's important to understand that repentance is a gift from God. It's not you beating yourself up to prove you're sorry. **Romans 2:4** reminds us not to overlook God's kindness, tolerance, and patience because it's this kindness from God that leads us to repentance.

"Repentance" simply means "to change your mind." It was a military term used to describe a marching soldier who did an about-face—stopping, turning, and proceeding in the opposite direction.

- **It's more than telling God you're sorry.**
- **It's more than a promise to stop your bad habits.**
- **It's more than a prayer you pray so you can enter heaven when you die.**

REPENTANCE

REPENTANCE IS

A TURNING FROM YOUR

OLD WAY OF THINKING:

FROM YOUR

SINFUL NATURE,

FROM SATISFYING YOUR

SELFISH DESIRES.

BUT IT'S ALSO

A TURNING TO:

TO A NEW LIFE

IN CHRIST,

TO A NEW WAY OF SEEING

YOURSELF AND OTHERS,

AND TO A

LIFE PRODUCING FRUIT

THAT HONORS GOD.

FOR ANSWERS TURN TO PAGES 154-155

According to 2 Corinthians 7:10, what do godly sorrow and repentance lead to?

Acts 26:20 makes it clear that true repentance is more than a private, internal change of heart. When repentance is genuine, when it comes from godly sorrow, what begins with a change in mind naturally produces a change in deeds. You don't just think differently; you act differently.

This has been the pattern from the very first followers of Jesus. In **Acts 2**, Peter preaches the first sermon after Jesus ascends to heaven and fills them with His power. There is a massive crowd of people gathered—we don't know how many were there, but we know about 3,000 people responded to Peter's message.

READ ACTS 2:36–39 AND ANSWER THE FOLLOWING QUESTIONS:

1. What did Peter mean when he told the people that they crucified Jesus? ***(verse 36)***

2. When Peter said, "this Jesus whom you crucified," it includes you. How were you responsible for Jesus' death? ***(verse 36)***

3. What happened to the people when they heard Peter's message? ***(verse 37)***

4. When the people asked, "Brothers, what shall we do?" what did Peter tell them? ***(verse 38)***

5. What gift were they promised in ***verse 38***?

FOR ANSWERS TURN TO PAGES 154-155

Throughout the book of Acts and the rest of the New Testament, there is a clear connection between repentance and baptism.

BAPTISM IS THE PUBLIC EXPRESSION OF THIS INWARD CHANGE.

When Jesus was baptized, God's voice could be heard declaring, **"YOU ARE MY SON, WHOM I LOVE; WITH YOU I AM WELL PLEASED" (Mark 1:11)**. When we put our trust in Jesus and receive His righteousness by faith, we receive the same approval from the Father.

Romans 6:3-4 describes baptism as a picture of sharing in both the death and burial of Jesus as well as His resurrection to a new life. Baptism does not make us right with God—Jesus' death and resurrection on our behalf accomplished this. Baptism is a public celebration of the joining of a believer to the power of what Jesus accomplished.

It's far more than a religious ceremony or tradition. It's an intentional, relational step of faith that lets the whole world know we're committed to Jesus and His new life at work in us.

Jesus told His followers to do two things with new disciples in **Matthew 28:19-20: (1)** baptize them and **(2)** teach them to obey everything He'd commanded.

Baptism is a one-time step of faith to celebrate genuine repentance to a new life in Christ.

Repentance begins as a one-time decision to turn your life of sin to a new life in Christ, but it is also the bedrock of a new way of living.

It is the daily commitment to change and obey as the Spirit of God leads and guides us. This is called the process of sanctification—the lifelong journey of becoming the person God created us to be as we continue to follow Jesus.

The natural, healthy response for a Christian who makes a poor choice is not to give up on their faith, to get re-baptized, or to question whether their relationship with God was ever genuine. It's simply to repent—to turn from the unhealthy thoughts, attitudes, and actions that move us away from Jesus and to move toward Him.

BAPTISM IS A ONE-TIME STEP OF FAITH TO CELEBRATE GENUINE REPENTANCE TO A NEW LIFE IN CHRIST.

REFLECT//DISCUSS

1. AFTER READING THIS CHAPTER, DO YOU FEEL LIKE YOU HAVE TRULY REPENTED OF SIN AND TURNED TO GOD? WHY OR WHY NOT?

2. WHAT ARE SOME UNHEALTHY THOUGHTS, ATTITUDES, OR ACTIONS THAT YOU STRUGGLE WITH? CONSIDER WRITING OUT A PRAYER IN THE SPACE BELOW, ASKING GOD TO HELP YOU OVERCOME THOSE AREAS.

3. IS WATER BAPTISM MORE THAN A TRADITIONAL RELIGIOUS CEREMONY? WHY?

4. SINCE REPENTING AND TURNING TO CHRIST, HAVE YOU BEEN BAPTIZED? IF SO, WHAT WAS THAT EXPERIENCE LIKE FOR YOU? IF NOT, WHAT IS HOLDING YOU BACK?

CHAPTER

1 WHAT AM I BUILDING MY LIFE ON?

2 HOW CAN I HAVE A RELATIONSHIP WITH GOD?

3 HOW DO I CHANGE AND BEGIN MY NEW LIFE IN CHRIST?

4 WHAT DOES GOD WANT FROM ME?

5 HOW DO I HEAR FROM GOD?

6 HOW CAN I EXPERIENCE GOD'S PRESENCE EVERY DAY?

7 WHERE HAS GOD PLACED ME?

8 HOW DOES GOD THINK ABOUT MONEY?

9 WHY IS THE CHURCH IMPORTANT?

10 WHAT DO I DO NOW?

CHAPTER 4

What Does God Want from Me?

LORDSHIP & OBEDIENCE

WRITE JOHN 14:15.

WRITE ACTS 2:36.

Once we put our trust in Jesus, repent from our sin, and publicly declare our faith in Him through baptism, ***what does God want from us next?***

The same thing He's always wanted:

OUR HEARTS.

FOR ANSWERS TURN TO PAGES 154-155

According to John 14:15, what does Jesus say is the way to show we love Him?

This is His "love language." We demonstrate our love for Him by becoming the person He created us to be through obeying what He has asked us to do.

People have called Jesus many things—a prophet, a wise teacher, a friend of sinners, the Son of God, Savior—but **Acts 2:36** tells us that God made Jesus "Lord." That's who He is whether we recognize it or not.

He doesn't say one thing and do another. He has perfect integrity. He's not a hypocrite—He used this term to describe someone who plays a role or acts like someone they're not.

JESUS CAN'T BE LESS THAN WHO HE IS.

In Peter's subsequent letter after his message in the book of Acts, he makes it clear that this is the expected response for all followers of Christ.

Jesus is more than a friend. He's more than a voice in our life. He's more than a ticket to heaven or someone we call when we're in trouble. Peter tells us to set Him apart (the definition of the word "sanctify" preferred by many translations) in our hearts as "Lord."

What does it mean to call someone Lord? In a literal sense, it means "master." It signifies authority, highest honor, and ultimate allegiance. In the ancient world, it was commonly used in the expression "Caesar is Lord," in recognition of the Roman Emperor as the leader of the world.

Therefore, a first-century person brazen enough to claim that "Jesus is Lord" was making a radical, potentially life-threatening statement. Thousands of the earliest Christ-followers paid the ultimate price for their faith—and this horrific practice still continues in restrictive nations to this day.

We may never face this level of sacrifice, but what does it mean for us to say that Jesus is Lord? How does it change our lives?

READ LUKE 6:46-49 AND ANSWER THE FOLLOWING QUESTIONS:

1.

What does Jesus expect of people who call Him "Lord"?
(verse 46)

2.

After we come to Jesus and hear His words, what does He expect us to do?
(verse 47)

3.

Which of the two men in this passage heard Jesus' words?

4.

What was the outcome for the man who built on the rock? ***(verse 48)***

5.

When does it say the house collapsed that was built on no foundation? ***(verse 49)***

FOR ANSWERS TURN TO PAGES 154-155

You probably noticed this is very similar to the **Matthew 7** passage we read in chapter one. This is Luke's version of that story. Luke starts with Jesus' question of lordship. Jesus is asking why someone would call Him "Lord" if they weren't willing to do what He says.

This may sound heavy. After all, who could possibly do what Jesus says at all times? We've already discovered that none of us could live up to this in order to earn a relationship with God.

So what is Jesus after?

Two of the most important words in this passage from Luke 6 are **"practice"** and **"foundation."** No one practices with perfect accuracy. Practice is the process of improvement, of changing your patterns based on repetition toward a clearly stated goal. In **1 John 3:10**, it says that the children of God are obvious because they practice righteousness.

This doesn't mean they're perfect in their obedience, but it does mean they're making clear progress. This concept is echoed throughout the New Testament.

The other significant word in this passage is "foundation." The foundation is a framework everything else is built on. It determines the shape and function of the rest of what follows. If the foundation of your life is that **"Jesus is a wise teacher,"** or **"Jesus is a friend,"** it will determine how you relate to Him.

IF YOU BUILD ON
THE FOUNDATION THAT
"JESUS IS LORD,"

IT MEANS THAT EVEN WHEN YOU
DON'T AGREE OR UNDERSTAND,

YOU COMMIT TO
FOLLOW AND OBEY.

If you build on the foundation that "Jesus is Lord," it means that even when you don't agree or understand, you commit to follow and obey.

It doesn't mean you'll always do everything perfectly, but it does mean you've chosen to give Him the final say.

"Lordship" scares us because it feels positional and impersonal. But when the Bible uses this concept, it's far more relational than we imagine.

We see a pattern throughout Scripture of God as a loving husband to His people:

- **Old Testament prophets – Ezekiel, Jeremiah, Isaiah, Hosea, and Joel**
- **Jesus in all four Gospels – Matthew, Mark, Luke, and John**
- **2 Corinthians**
- **Revelation**

But no other section uses it as clearly as **Ephesians 5**.

In this passage, God compares His relationship with His people to a husband and a wife. When a man and a woman exchange vows, they verbally commit to a covenant agreement saying, "I choose you above all others."

A marriage relationship is not contingent upon each person's ability to perfectly fulfill the other's expectations. They're making a promise to put each other first for the rest of their lives. It's not a partial commitment. It's not, "You can have my Friday to Sunday, but I can do whatever I want from Monday to Thursday."

We all grow in our ability to live this out, but if we have a genuine relationship with Jesus, we freely give up our right to say, "You can't have this area of my life."

Now the metaphor breaks down because in our relationships, neither party is perfect. But in our relationship with God, He perfectly fulfills and upholds His love for us. He doesn't expect us to reciprocate in our performance—but He does expect perfect faithfulness in our hearts.

The concepts of lordship and obedience cause us to hedge because we don't know if we can live up to them. Obedience motivated by obligation or guilt is weak. Obedience driven by a desire to live up to a perfect spiritual standard fades quickly.

LORDSHIP → LOVE → OBEDIENCE

If we have an obedience problem, we really have a love problem. We've lost our way. We've given our hearts to something else.

But in any of our most treasured relationships, the only lasting motivation is love. The same is true in our relationship with God. When we commit to putting Him first, when we offer our whole lives to Him out of love, we grow in our ability to obey and put His words into practice.

WHEN WE OFFER OUR WHOLE LIVES TO GOD OUT OF LOVE, WE GROW IN OUR ABILITY TO OBEY AND PUT HIS WORDS INTO PRACTICE.

REFLECT//DISCUSS

1. WHAT DOES IT MEAN TO MAKE JESUS YOUR "LORD"?

2. IN YOUR RELATIONSHIP WITH JESUS, DO YOU RELATE TO HIM AS SAVIOR? DO YOU KNOW HIM AS YOUR FRIEND? WHAT ABOUT LORD?

3. HAVE YOU GIVEN JESUS THE FINAL SAY IN YOUR LIFE? WHAT AREAS OF YOUR LIFE DO YOU STILL NEED TO SURRENDER TO GOD?

4. WHERE DOES THE MOTIVATION TO OBEY GOD'S COMMANDMENTS COME FROM? HOW DOES THIS CHANGE YOUR APPROACH?

CHAPTER

1 WHAT AM I BUILDING MY LIFE ON?

2 HOW CAN I HAVE A RELATIONSHIP WITH GOD?

3 HOW DO I CHANGE AND BEGIN MY NEW LIFE IN CHRIST?

4 WHAT DOES GOD WANT FROM ME?

5 HOW DO I HEAR FROM GOD?

6 HOW CAN I EXPERIENCE GOD'S PRESENCE EVERY DAY?

7 WHERE HAS GOD PLACED ME?

8 HOW DOES GOD THINK ABOUT MONEY?

9 WHY IS THE CHURCH IMPORTANT?

10 WHAT DO I DO NOW?

CHAPTER 5

How Do I Hear from God?

GOD'S WORD & SPIRITUAL HUNGER

WRITE 2 TIMOTHY 3:16.

WRITE HEBREWS 4:12.

Most people respect the Bible. Even if they don't agree with what Scripture says, they acknowledge the impact and influence of these 66 ancient books.

However, these same people also struggle to experience the living and active Word in their own lives. Despite our best intentions, Bible literacy has been steadily declining over the past few decades. There are several reasons for this.

THE BIBLE IS INTIMIDATING:

WHERE DO I START?

WHAT DOES IT MEAN?

HOW DOES IT FIT TOGETHER?

HOW DOES IT APPLY TO MY LIFE?

These are only a few of the most common challenges people encounter when they try to read it.

It's hard to understand, so you have to ask for help. This is often embarrassing, which also makes you want to set it aside and come back later. Another major problem is finding the time and attention to fully engage.

We're faced with a major dilemma: God says that all of His Word is alive and active; it's God-breathed and useful; it has the ability to judge the thoughts and attitudes of our hearts—but we don't know how to get those results.

How often do you read the Bible? Do you get much from it when you do?

The two biggest keys to getting over the obstacles preventing us from learning to hear God through His Word are

CONSISTENCY AND AUTHORITY.

↓

CONSISTENCY

IS CHOOSING TO READ THE BIBLE EVERY DAY
(EVEN FOR FIVE MINUTES).

↓

AUTHORITY

IS PREDETERMINING THAT WHEN YOU READ THE BIBLE
AND DON'T UNDERSTAND OR AGREE WITH SCRIPTURE,
YOU DON'T CHANGE IT—IT CHANGES YOU.

Here's the perspective shift that changes everything: The purpose of God's Word is not to study spiritual information, to prepare for an exam to get into heaven, or to memorize Bible trivia.

THE PURPOSE OF THE BIBLE IS TO SHOW US WHO GOD IS. IT'S RELATIONAL.

If God told you, **"I'm coming to spend 10 minutes with you to tell you what's on My heart,"** we'd all make time for Him. But this is precisely what He's done through His Word.

Maybe you've tried this. Maybe you're one of the many who started the "read the Bible in a year" plan and you got stuck on the side of the road in Leviticus. You're not alone. That group has a lot of members.

In our world today, we think important reading is personal, private, quiet, and solitary. This is not how the people of God read or studied Scripture throughout history. It was done in a group setting, with discussion, application, questions, and wrestling with concepts.

As we grow and learn how to do this together, we strengthen our ability to do it each day on our own—which only increases the quality of the discussions we have when we come back and talk about it together. It's not an either/or situation.

When a person gets excited about something, they study up and find a group of people who can help them grow in their understanding. Learning to hear God through His Word works the same way.

READ PSALM 19:7–14 AND ANSWER THE FOLLOWING QUESTIONS:

1. What are some of the different terms used for God's Word? ***(verses 7-9)***

2. What do the precepts and commands produce in ***verse 8***?

3. How valuable are the decrees of the Lord? ***(verses 9-10)***

FOR ANSWERS TURN TO PAGES 154-155

4. What advantages does ***verse 11*** promise?

5. What two things did the psalmist pray would be pleasing to the Lord?

The purpose of pleasing God with our words and our thoughts is relational.

We want to be close to Him more than we want to memorize information about Him. We want to live in a way that honors Him more than we want to prepare for an exam. When you're close to someone and your relationship is healthy, being with them is a privilege, not a burden or an obligation.

This is critical for lasting motivation. If we can't connect how reading the Bible brings us into a deeper relationship with God, we'll give up. But once we learn how to find God's voice in His Word, we'll make time to be with Him every day.

Jesus placed such incredible value on being close with His Father. He told the disciples on multiple occasions that it was more vital than food for our survival.

We've all struggled to understand what God's voice sounds like. No one has a special hotline to God.

If we want to know what God thinks, if we want to know what He sounds like, if we want to know how to recognize His voice out of the thoughts running through our minds, then we start with His Word.

Joshua 1:8 explains that if we talk about and think about God's Word every day, we will be able to do what it says—which will cause us to be successful. **James 1:22** reminds us not to just hear the Word but also to do what it says.

It's not about how much of the Bible you know; it's about how much of the Bible you can actually live.

BOOKS OF THE BIBLE

OLD TESTAMENT

GENESIS
EXODUS
LEVITICUS
NUMBERS
DEUTERONOMY
JOSHUA
JUDGES
RUTH
1 SAMUEL
2 SAMUEL
1 KINGS
2 KINGS
1 CHRONICLES
2 CHRONICLES
EZRA
NEHEMIAH
ESTHER
JOB
PSALMS
PROVERBS
ECCLESIASTES
SONG OF SOLOMON
ISAIAH
JEREMIAH
LAMENTATIONS
EZEKIEL
DANIEL
HOSEA
JOEL
AMOS
OBADIAH
JONAH
MICAH
NAHUM
HABAKKUK
ZEPHANIAH
HAGGAI
ZECHARIAH
MALACHI

NEW TESTAMENT

→ **MATTHEW**
→ **MARK**
→ **LUKE**
→ **JOHN**

(MATTHEW, MARK, LUKE, JOHN — THE GOSPELS)

ACTS
ROMANS
1 CORINTHIANS
2 CORINTHIANS
GALATIANS
EPHESIANS
PHILIPPIANS
COLOSSIANS
1 THESSALONIANS
2 THESSALONIANS
1 TIMOTHY
2 TIMOTHY
TITUS
PHILEMON
HEBREWS
JAMES
1 PETER
2 PETER
1 JOHN
2 JOHN
3 JOHN
JUDE
REVELATION

REFLECT//DISCUSS

1. THE PURPOSE OF READING THE BIBLE IS RELATIONAL. HOW DOES THAT CHANGE YOUR PERSPECTIVE ON GOD'S WORD?

2. DO YOU HAVE PEOPLE YOU COULD START READING THE BIBLE WITH? WRITE OUT ONE OR TWO NAMES AND REACH OUT TO THEM THIS WEEK.

3. WHAT IS THE GREATEST CHALLENGE YOU FACE IN TRYING TO HEAR GOD THROUGH HIS WORD ON A DAILY BASIS (DON'T UNDERSTAND, DON'T HAVE TIME, ETC.)?

4. HOW DOES THE BIBLE IMPACT THE WAY YOU SPEAK AND THE WAY YOU THINK? GIVE A SPECIFIC EXAMPLE.

5. CAN YOU THINK OF A SPECIFIC MORAL ISSUE WHERE YOU CHANGED YOUR MIND BECAUSE OF WHAT THE BIBLE SAYS? HOW DID IT IMPACT YOUR DAILY LIFE?

CHAPTER

CHAPTER 6

How Can I Experience God's Presence Every Day?

THE HOLY SPIRIT & SPIRITUAL GIFTS

WRITE LUKE 11:13.

WRITE ACTS 1:8.

WRITE ACTS 2:38-39.

You want to grow closer to God—your choice to read this book is a clear demonstration of this desire. And a significant part of growing closer to God includes a relationship with the Holy Spirit.

We want this, but so many people wrestle with how it works. We can grasp the concept of God. We can relate to Jesus. But the Holy Spirit often feels like something totally different.

IF WE WANT A RELATIONSHIP WITH THE HOLY SPIRIT, THE PLACE WE NEED TO START, THE STANDARD WE NEED TO LOOK TO, IS THE WORD OF GOD.

In **John 16:7**, Jesus told His disciples it was to their advantage that He left them to go to His Father. Why would He make such an outrageous claim? Because He knew His absence would lead His Father to send them the Holy Spirit. Later in the same passage, Jesus said the Holy Spirit would lead and guide them into all truth **(see John 16:13)**.

The verses at the beginning of the chapter reinforce this radical idea, but they also make it clear that we're included in this amazing promise. We can have the same advantage they had.

Jesus said that our heavenly Father will give the Holy Spirit to any of His children who simply ask Him.

Jesus told the disciples the Holy Spirit wouldn't just give them information; the Holy Spirit would give them the power to tell the whole world about Him.

And in his first message, Peter reminds us that the gift of the Holy Spirit is not merely for pastors, ministry leaders, or some kind of super Christians.

According to Acts 2:39, who is God's promise of the Holy Spirit for?

JESUS SAID THAT OUR HEAVENLY FATHER WILL GIVE THE HOLY SPIRIT TO ANY OF HIS CHILDREN WHO SIMPLY ASK HIM.

FOR ANSWERS TURN TO PAGES 154-155

FIVE FOUNDATIONAL TRUTHS ABOUT THE HOLY SPIRIT

01 02 03 04

1 HE IS THE THIRD PERSON OF THE TRINITY.

2 HE IS GOD.

3 HE IS A PERSON.

4 HE IS ACTIVE AND WORKING IN THE WORLD.

05

5 HIS ROLES INCLUDE:

- **HELPER** WHO TEACHES/REMINDS **(JOHN 14:26)**
- **GUIDE** WHO LEADS TO ALL TRUTH **(JOHN 16:13)**
- **ADVOCATE** WHO CONVICTS THE WORLD OF SIN **(JOHN 16:7-8)**
- **GIVER** OF SPIRITUAL GIFTS **(1 CORINTHIANS 12:7-11; ROMANS 12:6-8)**
- **SANCTIFIER** WHO EMPOWERS GOOD FRUIT IN OUR LIVES **(GALATIANS 5:22-25; ACTS 1:8)**

Jesus' most exhaustive teaching on the Holy Spirit **(see John 14–17, often called the Farewell Discourse)** takes place immediately following the Last Supper on the night before He was crucified. He was preparing His closest friends to experience God's presence in their lives on a daily basis—and in doing so, He prepares all of us who follow Him to do the same.

READ JOHN 14:15-17, 25-27 AND ANSWER THE FOLLOWING QUESTIONS:

1.

What is the first thing Jesus calls the Holy Spirit in ***verse 16***?

2.

What are the first two things He does? ***(verse 16)***

3.

Who does Jesus say cannot accept the Holy Spirit, and why? ***(verse 17)***

4.

According to the end of ***verse 17***, how do we know the Holy Spirit?

5.

What does Jesus say the Holy Spirit will do for us in ***verse 26***?

FOR ANSWERS TURN TO PAGES 154-155

↓

THREE KEY CONTRIBUTIONS
FROM THE HOLY SPIRIT:

↓

1. THE FRUIT OF THE SPIRIT

Galatians 5:22-23 describes the fruit of the Holy Spirit as love, joy, peace, forbearance, kindness, goodness, faithfulness, gentleness, and self-control. The good news is, these don't grow out of our lives through discipline and willpower; they show up when we live under the influence and guidance of the Holy Spirit.

2. THE GIFTS OF THE SPIRIT

Romans 12:5-8 tells us we've been given different gifts through the Spirit, not for our own benefit, but to add value to each other **(see 1 Corinthians 12:7-11, 27-31, and Ephesians 4:11-12)**.

The important principle is to discover your gifts and to use them to serve others—Peter makes this clear in **1 Peter 4:10-11**. When this happens, others benefit from your gift, you receive fulfillment, and God receives glory.

3. THE BAPTISM WITH THE HOLY SPIRIT

The Bible is clear: The Holy Spirit comes and lives inside you at the moment of salvation. But all throughout the New Testament, we see a subsequent interaction with the Holy Spirit. In **Acts 1:5**, Jesus tells His disciples that John baptized them with water but later they would be baptized with the Holy Spirit. And then throughout the book of **Acts (chapters 8, 10, 11, and 19)**, we see this process repeated in the lives of followers of Christ.

If we summarize how Jesus led the disciples to relate to the Holy Spirit, we see a pattern of prayer, power, continual filling, and a boldness to speak the Word. That's what He trained them to expect.

Remember, JUSTIFICATION happens in a moment. We can't earn it. We receive salvation as a gift from God. Nothing needs to be added for us to be right with God.

The process of SANCTIFICATION is where we become more and more like Him. It doesn't make us right with God, but it is how we grow. One of the primary catalysts of this process is the ongoing and empowering work of the Holy Spirit.

Ephesians 5:18-20 tells us to be filled with the Spirit as we encourage and speak to one another through songs and with grateful hearts to God. The word used in verse 18 may be better understood as an ongoing filling. It's not a one-time event.

The Bible tells us that the baptism with the Holy Spirit is a gift that gives us the help, the power, and the filling Jesus promised to anyone who simply asks.

THE BAPTISM WITH THE HOLY SPIRIT IS A GIFT THAT GIVES US THE HELP, THE POWER, AND THE FILLING JESUS **PROMISED TO ANYONE WHO SIMPLY ASKS.**

REFLECT// DISCUSS

1. READ THE LIST OF THE FRUIT OF THE SPIRIT IN GALATIANS 5:22-23. ARE THERE ANY AREAS FROM THIS LIST THAT YOU WOULD LIKE TO GROW IN? HOW CAN YOU GROW IN THESE AREAS?

2. DO YOU KNOW WHAT YOUR SPIRITUAL GIFTS ARE? IF SO, WRITE THEM OUT HERE. IF YOU DON'T, HOW CAN YOU DISCOVER AND DEVELOP THEM?

3. WHAT IS THE PURPOSE OF SPIRITUAL GIFTS?

4. HOW OFTEN DO YOU SEEK THE INFILLING PRESENCE OF THE HOLY SPIRIT IN YOUR LIFE? IS THIS AN AREA YOU WOULD LIKE TO GROW IN? EXPLAIN.

5. HAVE YOU EVER STRUGGLED TO RELATE TO THE HOLY SPIRIT? IF YES, YOU'RE DEFINITELY NOT ALONE. WHAT HAS MADE IT DIFFICULT FOR YOU?

CHAPTER

CHAPTER 7

Where Has God Placed Me?

CONNECTION & SPIRITUAL FAMILY

WRITE PSALM 68:6.

WRITE 1 CORINTHIANS 12:18.

CHAPTER 7

YOU'RE ON A JOURNEY WITH GOD.

You're developing your spiritual foundations. You may be asking, "What do I do now?" Here are a few (but not all) of the options available to you:

A. **Make it up as you go along based on what feels right to you.**

B. **Hop around to different groups, friends, and churches until you find the perfect place that meets all your needs.**

C. **Put it off until later.**

D. **Commit to where God has placed you.**

The problem with options A, B, and C is that we separate ourselves as the decision maker. **Proverbs 18:1** warns us, **"He who separates himself seeks his own desire; he quarrels against all sound wisdom" (NASB)**.

A common mistake people often make early in their spiritual development is to think, *it's just me and Jesus.* But Jesus said that starting a genuine relationship with Him was like being born again. No one leaves a baby on their own—it's cared for and grows in the context of a loving family.

Let's look at the two verses at the start of this chapter. Consider God's wisdom in **Psalm 68:6** and **1 Corinthians 12:18** in choosing to commit to where God has placed you.

WHEN YOU GIVE YOUR LIFE TO CHRIST, WHEN YOU'RE ADOPTED INTO THE KINGDOM OF GOD, HE SETS YOU IN HIS FAMILY.

Many of us have had incredibly painful challenges with our natural families, so it's hard for us to accept, but spiritual family is absolutely one of the most significant blessings God gives us.

God loved you while you were disobedient to Him. He cared for you while you were His enemy. He loves you enough to have sent His Son, Jesus, to die on the cross to bring you home. Then after all that, why wouldn't He have a place prepared just for you?

God knows the details of your life. He has a place designed for you to grow, and because God builds according to the pattern of family, that place is a church home.

THIS IS SPIRITUAL FAMILY — IT'S A COMMITMENT TO THE DIVINE RELATIONSHIPS GOD PLACES IN YOUR LIFE.

Spiritual family is God's idea.

It's not a style of church. It's more than friendly people who are excited about their church. It's a revelation, a conviction, a biblical pattern of the way God builds.

↓

GOD BUILDS THROUGH FAMILY
(BOTH NATURAL AND SPIRITUAL)

↓

ADAM AND EVE - GENESIS 1–5

- Adam and Eve were God's first children and design.
- This family unit was Satan's first target of attack.
- Within a few generations, they had forgotten their covenant and relationship with God.

NOAH - GENESIS 5–10

- The world became corrupt and evil. No man followed God except for one—Noah.
- God flooded the earth and began again with Noah and his family.
- God made a covenant with Noah never to flood the earth again.

ABRAHAM - GENESIS 11–31

- God promised a childless 100-year-old man named Abram that he would father a nation more plentiful than the stars in the sky.
- God changed his name to Abraham, and God was faithful to give him a son, Isaac.
- Through Isaac and his son Jacob, Abraham fathered the tribes of Israel—God's chosen people.

RUTH AND NAOMI - RUTH

- Ruth, a Moabite widow, makes a covenant to care for her mother-in-law, who was also widowed, during a famine.
- God honors this covenant and brings Ruth an honorable Israelite husband, Boaz. She became a great-grandmother of King David.

DAVID - 1 & 2 SAMUEL; 1 & 2 CHRONICLES

- David was mistreated by his family but saves his people by defeating Goliath. This propels him in line to the throne of Israel.
- The current king, Saul, is jealous of David, and attempts to kill him.
- Jonathan, Saul's son, is the rightful heir to the throne, but Jonathan protects David because he believes David is spiritual family.

JESUS - THE GOSPELS

- Centuries later, Jesus, Son of God and descendant of David, is born.
- Jesus loved and served His natural family, but He believed His brothers and sisters also included those who did the will of God.
- Jesus told His disciples He loved them the way the Father loved Him. He called them His friends.

PAUL/EARLY CHURCH - ACTS & NEW TESTAMENT LETTERS

- The idea of spiritual family in the early church was passed down from Jesus' relationships with His disciples.
- Paul often used familial language (brother, sister, son, daughter) to describe unrelated members of church families.

GOD SETS THE LONELY IN FAMILIES.

PSALM 68:6a

READ ACTS 2:42–47 AND ANSWER THE FOLLOWING QUESTIONS:

1.

What were the four things the first followers of Jesus devoted themselves to? ***(verse 42)***

2.

According to ***verse 43,*** what was everyone filled with?

3.

Were they selfish and focused on their own needs? What were they focused on? ***(verses 44-45)***

4.

How does ***verse 46*** describe their hearts?

5.

Who did the Lord add to their number daily? ***(verse 47)***

FOR ANSWERS TURN TO PAGES 154-155

The early church wasn't perfect—God made significant changes to the way they did ministry all throughout the book of Acts. But one thing they got right from the very beginning was the idea of spiritual family. These were not people without problems, but this was an atmosphere where they were enjoying every day they spent with God and each other.

They didn't come up with this on their own—they simply repeated what they had learned from Jesus.

The church was creating a big stir and the Jewish leaders and elders called Peter and John in to investigate what was going on. **Acts 4:13** tells us that these highly educated religious leaders were astonished because

PETER AND JOHN WERE ORDINARY AND UNSCHOOLED, BUT EVERYONE KNEW THEY HAD BEEN WITH JESUS.

This approach continued to spread. It became normal in the early church for Christians to call each other brothers and sisters. Family language was everywhere. The apostle Paul called his disciple Timothy his beloved son in the faith.

↓

WHAT DOES IT MEAN TO BE
A PART OF SPIRITUAL FAMILY?

↓

1. YOU BELIEVE GOD PLACED YOU IN THE FAMILY.

This may seem strange, but we don't choose our natural family either. It's a divine joining, not a disposable or transactional relationship. How you treat your spiritual family is a direct reflection of how you treat God.

If you don't have a clear sense that God placed you in your church, then you need to find out why. You're going to have a hard time benefitting from spiritual family if you're constantly wavering over whether or not you believe you're where God set you.

2. YOU DISCOVER AND DEVELOP YOUR GIFTS IN THE CONTEXT OF FAMILY.

Family is the most natural environment for growth and development. That's what families do. In a family, people find interests, receive feedback and coaching, provide support and opportunities, and discover talents and abilities. The process takes time and patience, but it also requires close proximity and honest relationships.

3. YOU USE YOUR GIFTS TO SERVE THE FAMILY.

In a healthy family, no one sits back and watches. You jump in and offer your part. You can't do everything, but you're grateful to contribute whatever you can because you believe that when any part of the family wins, every part of the family celebrates.

4. YOU PUT THE NEEDS AND THE GOALS OF THE FAMILY AHEAD OF YOUR OWN.

This sounds like a guaranteed way to get less, but the truth is, our greatest fulfillment in life is found in helping someone else win. Jesus said that the greatest is the servant, that it's better to give than to receive; and His disciple John said that there's no greater joy than watching your children walk in the truth. John was writing to a church when he said it because he was talking about spiritual family.

REFLECT // DISCUSS

1. LOOK AT THE FOUR OPTIONS ON PAGE 97. WHICH ONE OF THESE BEST DESCRIBES YOU? EXPLAIN.

2. HOW DOES KNOWING THAT GOD HAS PLANTED YOU IN YOUR CHURCH HELP YOU IN THE LONG TERM? DO YOU FEEL PLANTED IN YOUR CHURCH?

3. ARE YOU ACTIVELY SERVING AND USING YOUR GIFTS IN YOUR CHURCH? WHY OR WHY NOT?

4. WHAT HAPPENS TO US WHEN WE GIVE OUR LIVES TO JESUS? DOES IT JUST BECOME "YOU AND GOD"? EXPLAIN.

5. HAVE YOU EVER EXPERIENCED SPIRITUAL FAMILY? IF NOT, WOULD YOU LIKE TO? WHAT HAS HELD YOU BACK FROM IT?

CHAPTER

1 WHAT AM I BUILDING MY LIFE ON?

2 HOW CAN I HAVE A RELATIONSHIP WITH GOD?

3 HOW DO I CHANGE AND BEGIN MY NEW LIFE IN CHRIST?

4 WHAT DOES GOD WANT FROM ME?

5 HOW DO I HEAR FROM GOD?

6 HOW CAN I EXPERIENCE GOD'S PRESENCE EVERY DAY?

7 WHERE HAS GOD PLACED ME?

8 HOW DOES GOD THINK ABOUT MONEY?

9 WHY IS THE CHURCH IMPORTANT?

10 WHAT DO I DO NOW?

CHAPTER 8
How Does God Think About Money?

STEWARDSHIP, GIVING, & GENEROSITY

WRITE PROVERBS 3:9-10.

WRITE MATTHEW 6:21.

God is infinite and uncreated.
He does not need anything.
He is the source.
He is the author of life and the giver
of every good and perfect gift.

He certainly does not need your money. But because He loves you, He cares about what you do with your money. **Proverbs 3** challenges us to honor God with our money. It also comes with a promise that **this way of life leads to more provision.**

In **Matthew 6:21**, Jesus tells us that wherever our money goes, our hearts will follow. In the two previous verses, Jesus contrasts people who spend their money filling up storehouses on earth with people who give generously for the purposes of heaven.

A pattern seen throughout Scripture is that when we are faithful to God's will, He is faithful to increase and bless our efforts, relationships, finances, and every aspect of life. That concept is called stewardship.

BECAUSE GOD LOVES YOU, HE CARES ABOUT WHAT YOU DO WITH YOUR MONEY.

STEWARDSHIP BEGINS BY UNDERSTANDING THAT EVERYTHING BELONGS TO GOD.

LOOK UP PSALM 24:1.

↓

What does this verse say about the world and its contents/inhabitants?

The reality is, every gift, talent, and resource we have was entrusted to us by a generous God:

- God gave us life.
- God created our minds and the creative ideas they produce.
- God created us with abilities that allow us to accumulate resources.
- God created the world for us to enjoy and thrive in.

When we understand that our money, time, and talents belong to God, it changes how we look at our resources. God honors hard work. There is inherent value in both discipline and diligence. But not a single one of us is self-made or truly owns what we have.

One day, our time on this earth will come to an end and we won't take anything with us. What we have acquired will be divided up and given away.

Being a steward means asking the question, "How can I honor God with what He has given me?" This is the opposite of how our world operates.

FOR ANSWERS TURN TO PAGES 154-155

WHEN WE TRULY GRASP THAT WE ARE STEWARDING GOD'S RESOURCES, WE SEE THE ABILITY TO MAKE MONEY AS A GIFT FROM GOD.

Money is an amazing tool that can provide an amazing life for ourselves and our families. Money allows us to give to those in need, honor God with our resources, and enjoy the amazing things He has placed in our lives. But when money becomes the source of our identity, hope, and purpose, it becomes a terrible god.

FOR ANSWERS TURN TO PAGES 154-155

LOOK UP 1 TIMOTHY 6:10.

↓

What does this verse say about the love of money?

Notice that **1 Timothy 6:10** doesn't say that money is evil, just the love of it. This same idea is echoed in another place in Scripture, except here, Jesus takes it one step further.

READ MATTHEW 6:24–34 AND ANSWER THE FOLLOWING QUESTIONS:

1. Does Jesus say it's possible to serve two masters? Who are the two masters we must choose between? ***(verse 24)***

2. What does Jesus say about worry in ***verse 25***?

3. What does Jesus say people are more valuable than? ***(verse 26)***

4. In ***verse 33,*** what does Jesus tell us to seek first? What happens when we do that?

5. In ***verse 34***, Jesus says not to worry about tomorrow. What reasons does He give?

FOR ANSWERS TURN TO PAGES 154–155

Notice what Jesus is saying in this passage. You only get one option. You cannot serve both God and money. One of them has to come first. One of them ends up serving the other.

If money is your god, money has the final say in your worth, significance, priorities, and life. But when you trust God as your source, you put your hope in Him and His Kingdom before your worries about your provision. God is not looking for a reason to make you suffer or to give you less. He loves you and He knows what you need.

We can easily feel that the resources and blessings in our lives are a product of our own efforts. Jesus shows us in the **Matthew 6** passage that we should not worry about being provided for, and that when we seek God's Kingdom and trust Him as our source, the resources and needs we have will be faithfully met by His goodness.

BECAUSE GOD WANTS OUR HEARTS TO BE CLOSE TO HIM, BECAUSE HE WANTS TO BUILD OUR TRUST AND CONFIDENCE IN HIM AS OUR SOURCE, BECAUSE HE WANTS US TO GROW IN OUR STEWARDSHIP AND GENEROSITY, HE COMMANDS US TO TITHE.

You may have never heard this word before. "Tithe" simply means "tenth." The tithe is the first 10 percent of earnings, profits, or increase in resources returned to God. It is the first step in honoring God with our finances. Our tithe goes to our local church, the family of believers where God has planted us.

The easiest way to learn this principle is to start early—the smaller the amount the easier it is to apply it. Young kids can tithe from their allowance. As teenagers get their first job or begin to earn income, tithing becomes a way to continue to trust God and build their faith. If you don't have income, you don't have a tithe, but you can still be generous with what you have. No matter how old you are, it comes back to your heart, and it's never too late to start.

Whatever is first in our budget is first in our hearts. It's a position of honor. This is what **Proverbs 3:9** means by "firstfruits."

LOOK UP LEVITICUS 27:30.

↓

What does this verse say about the tithe?

FOR ANSWERS TURN TO PAGES 154-155

When we tithe, we acknowledge it belongs to the Lord, like everything else in our lives. The tithe is one of the most basic steps in our stewardship development process. As we read in **Matthew 6:21**, God knows that our heart follows our treasure, and our heart is what God desires.

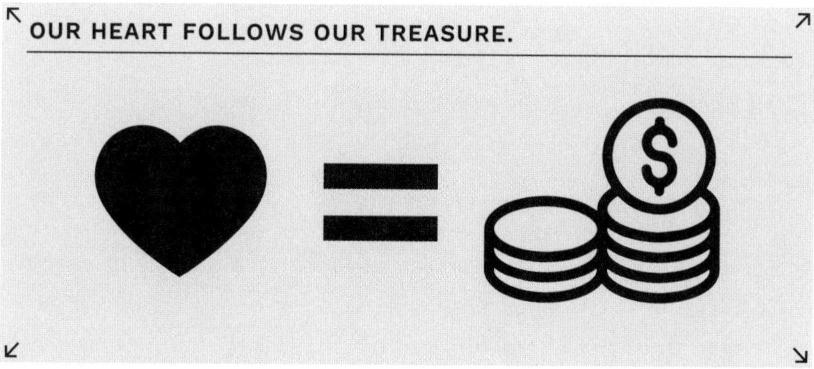

Some people try to dismiss the tithe as an Old Testament law, but Abraham and Jacob both tithed long before Moses was alive or God gave him the Ten Commandments **(see Genesis 14:20; 28:20-22)**. Jesus affirmed the tithe as a starting place for our generosity, and He consistently elevated Old Testament commands **(see Matthew 23:23; Luke 11:42)**.

Others suggest the church cares too much about money, but Jesus talked about handling resources in a way that honors God as much as He talked about any subject. Every healthy church takes care of people, and this is a function of stewardship.

For most people, the objections to tithing are more practical. It's much easier to be conveniently ignorant and act like we don't know. It's difficult to start later in life because we're managing more—we have to overcome our fear and trust God to do what He said He'd do.

In **Luke 16:10**, Jesus teaches that whoever is faithful with little can be trusted with more. **Malachi 3:10** says, **"'Bring the whole tithe into the storehouse, that there may be food in my house. Test me in this,' says the LORD Almighty, 'and see if I will not throw open the floodgates of heaven and pour out so much blessing that there will not be room enough to store it.'"**

Tithing reinforces our trust in God as our source, it demonstrates we love Him more than money, it builds our confidence, and it increases our affection and priority for God's Church.

But God's desire for us goes beyond honoring Him with our resources and being good stewards. His plan for each of us is to be like Him—generous in every way.

Mature, generous believers understand that the tithe is the minimum; it's the starting point. True generosity comes on top of our faithful obedience in returning to God the first 10 percent of everything He has so generously given us.

TITHING REINFORCES OUR TRUST IN GOD AS OUR SOURCE. IT DEMONSTRATES **WE LOVE HIM MORE THAN MONEY...HIS PLAN FOR EACH OF US IS TO BE LIKE HIM—GENEROUS IN EVERY WAY.**

READ 2 CORINTHIANS 9:7–11 AND ANSWER THE FOLLOWING QUESTIONS:

FOR ANSWERS TURN TO PAGES 154-155

1.

Does God want us to be reluctant or manipulated into giving? What kind of giver does God love? ***(verse 7)***

2.

According to ***verse 10***, what does God give to sowers? What do you do with seed?

3.

In what ways will God enrich us? When can we be generous? What happens when we're generous? ***(verse 11)***

The goal of building our lives on the foundation of Jesus is not to learn more information—it's to live like Jesus lived. And we can't live like Jesus without being generous.

Generosity includes our time, our talent, and our treasure. During different seasons of our lives, we have a greater ability to give out of different categories. We can bless others and honor God when we give out of any of them, but a generous spirit doesn't look for the most convenient option.

Jesus gave everything. He didn't hold back. He didn't only give to those who deserved it. He wasn't concerned with what He could get. He was always looking for ways to serve and give to others.

He wants us to have this same spirit. When we have a generous spirit, we live openhanded to give and invest in others. We're always looking for new ways to bless others. We don't have a scarcity mindset that's focused on ways to give less. We have an abundance mindset constantly devising new ways to be generous. And people with a generous spirit experience a life with more joy, blessing, and meaning.

REFLECT// DISCUSS

1. DO YOU BELIEVE THAT EVERYTHING YOU HAVE COMES FROM GOD? WHAT MAKES THIS DIFFICULT?

2. HAVE YOU EVER THOUGHT OF YOURSELF AS A STEWARD? HOW DOES THIS CONCEPT OF "STEWARDSHIP" CHANGE YOUR RELATIONSHIP WITH GOD?

3. WHAT IS THE BIGGEST OBSTACLE THAT COULD KEEP YOU FROM TITHING?

4. READ MATTHEW 6:33 AGAIN. TAKE A MOMENT TO ASK YOURSELF, "DO I REALLY BELIEVE GOD WILL PROVIDE EVERYTHING I NEED?"

5. WHICH AREA OF GENEROSITY (TIME, TALENT, TREASURE) IS THE EASIEST FOR YOU TO GIVE? WHAT'S THE MOST DIFFICULT?

CHAPTER

1 WHAT AM I BUILDING MY LIFE ON?

2 HOW CAN I HAVE A RELATIONSHIP WITH GOD?

3 HOW DO I CHANGE AND BEGIN MY NEW LIFE IN CHRIST?

4 WHAT DOES GOD WANT FROM ME?

5 HOW DO I HEAR FROM GOD?

6 HOW CAN I EXPERIENCE GOD'S PRESENCE EVERY DAY?

7 WHERE HAS GOD PLACED ME?

8 HOW DOES GOD THINK ABOUT MONEY?

9 WHY IS THE CHURCH IMPORTANT?

10 WHAT IS THE GOAL OF THE CHRISTIAN LIFE?

CHAPTER 9

Why Is the Church Important?

GOD'S PURPOSE & GOD'S PEOPLE

WRITE EPHESIANS 5:25.

WRITE HEBREWS 10:24-25.

If we're going to build our lives on Jesus, we have to love what He loves. **Ephesians 5:25** shows us that Jesus loves the Church the way a husband is meant to love his wife—he gives himself up; he honors, serves, loves, and leads her.

JESUS REALLY LOVES HIS CHURCH, AND HE WANTS US TO LOVE HIS CHURCH THE WAY WE LOVE HIM.

When the Bible talks about the Church, it's not talking about a building, a religious service, or a denomination.

THE CHURCH IS NOT A BUILDING—IT'S THE PEOPLE OF GOD.

The word "church" literally translates to "called-out ones." God's Church is His people, set apart to serve and love those around them. People are the common denominator. We are His Church—God's people gathered together in God's name, to reflect His image to the world, to carry out His mission, to reach people and build lives. **Hebrews 10:24-25** tells us that we are to spur one another on in love and good deeds, not giving up meeting together, but encouraging one another—more and more as the days go on.

God's Church is the representation of His Kingdom in the earth. It's His family—His chosen people to reflect His love to the world. It's also His body—His hands and feet that allow a skeptical world to see and know Him.

But the Church is also the place where we make friends, grow in our relationship with God, and use our gifts to love and serve people. And not just us. Our kids. Our parents. Our grandparents. We're never too old or too young. Every generation is included in reaching people and building lives.

GOD'S CHURCH IS HIS PEOPLE, SET APART TO SERVE AND LOVE THOSE AROUND THEM.

Different scholars have different opinions on when the Church started. Some say it was when Peter preached the first message by the disciples and thousands of people were saved in **Acts 2**. Others say it happened in **Matthew 16**.

In that story, Jesus asked the disciples who people said He was. Then He asked them what they thought. When Peter said Jesus was the Christ, the Son of the living God, Jesus called Peter blessed and said no person could have given him that answer.

And then Jesus told Peter that on this revelation—this understanding of Jesus as the Son of God—He would build His Church, and the gates of hell would not prevail against it.

Jesus never promised to build a religion. He didn't promise to build a brand. He only promised to build one thing. The thing He cares about the most—His Church.

Jesus is the head of the Church; He's the Chief Shepherd; He has first place in everything. But He invites us into His mission. He has a part for each of us to play in redeeming and restoring all of creation to the glory of the Father.

READ EPHESIANS 4:11–16 AND ANSWER THE FOLLOWING QUESTIONS:

1. What do the specific roles (evangelists, pastors, teachers, etc.) in ***verse 11*** all work together to do in ***verse 12***?

2. What happens when the people work and serve? ***(verse 13)***

3. What things cause people who are not mature in their faith to be tossed back and forth and blown here and there? ***(verse 14)***

4. How are we instructed to speak the truth? What happens when we do that? ***(verse 15)***

5. What happens to the Church when every part does its work? ***(verse 16)***

FOR ANSWERS TURN TO PAGES 154-155

Paul is writing to the church in Ephesus. It was a large church having a major impact on the entire region. Think about the summary of what Paul has said. The people in full-time ministry (pastors, teachers, etc.) equip people in the church for works of service. In other words, no matter what our job is, we're all in ministry. We're all in the game. All of us have something to offer.

What happens when Jesus builds the Church?

- **It gets mature and healthy.**
- **It's not easily distracted.**
- **It speaks the truth in love.**
- **It grows and builds itself up in love.**
- **It looks like Jesus.**

You may have never thought of church this way. Like so many others, you may have had disappointments, unmet expectations, or a bad experience in church. Because churches are made up of imperfect people, there is no perfect church. And yet God has not abandoned His plan.

Are there hypocrites in churches? Of course. There are also hypocrites in every workplace, every classroom, every gym, every hobby group, and every family. Everywhere you find people, you will eventually experience the pain that results from people who do not keep their word or treat others with kindness.

Remember, Jesus puts the ultimate responsibility for the success of the Church on Himself. His track record speaks volumes. Over the past two thousand years, despite all the mistakes human beings have made, God's Church keeps moving forward, transforming lives and changing the world.

Global political and military empires rise and fall. Fortune 500 companies come and go. But the Church endures because of Jesus.

FOR ANSWERS TURN TO PAGES 154-155

Look up Ephesians 3:10.

↓

What happens through the Church, according to this verse?

God doesn't speak to one kind of person. He speaks to everyone. The word "manifold" in verse 10 means "multifaceted." Think of it like the entire color spectrum. When God's Church comes together in all of its beautiful expressions, His enemies (rulers and authorities in the heavenly realms) hear the wisdom of God through the Church.

When it's healthy, the local church is the most resource-rich environment on the planet. It's the one place where people from every background, every generation, every cultural and ethnic heritage, and every diverse skill and ability come together to form a family.

God designed His Church to function like a family. Everyone starts with, "I'm going to set aside my needs for the sake of loving and serving others."

IN AN EVERYONE CHURCH, PEOPLE ARE:

LOVED AND WELCOMED

EXCITED AND ENGAGED

GROWING AND USING GIFTS

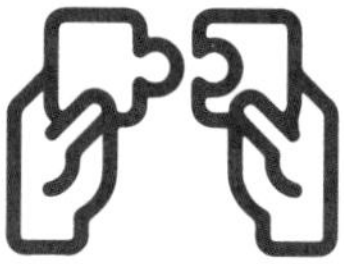

CONTRIBUTING AND SERVING OTHERS

DEVELOPED AND DISCIPLED

In an everyone church, behind these friendly, engaged, generous people is a loving Father always working to welcome new people into His family.

It's more than a building, a program, or an event. When God's people gather together in His name to welcome others, this environment becomes the most naturally evangelistic setting in the world.

This requires a perspective shift. If you view the church as a mildly beneficial option you attend when you have a free weekend, then you won't ever come close to receiving what God created you for.

But when you see how important it truly is, you move from a casual observer to a contributor. You stop thinking about your preferences and desires and instead you think about how you can be part of what God is doing. Your relationship with God grows. You experience church differently.

YOU DEVELOP CHARACTER AS YOU WALK WITH MATURE BELIEVERS.

YOU LEARN HUMILITY FROM TRUSTED RELATIONSHIPS.

YOU EXPERIENCE GOD'S PRESENCE AS YOU PRIORITIZE HIS PURPOSE.

YOU RECEIVE WISDOM FROM PEOPLE WHO ARE GIFTED IN WAYS YOU'RE NOT.

YOU DISCOVER OPPORTUNITIES TO SERVE, WHICH MAKES YOU MORE GENEROUS.

YOU BECOME A MORE EFFECTIVE LEADER AT HOME AND IN YOUR WORKPLACE.

This doesn't even take into account how it impacts the rest of your family. The starting place for all of this is the shift from "What do I get out of this?" to "How can I serve someone else?"

THIS IS THE POWER OF THE CHURCH.

REFLECT// DISCUSS

1. WHAT DOES THE WORD "CHURCH" MEAN? IS IT MORE ABOUT A BUILDING AND SERVICES, OR IS IT ABOUT THE PEOPLE? EXPLAIN.

2. WHAT HAPPENS IN A CHURCH WHEN EVERY PERSON OFFERS THEIR GIFTS AND DOES THEIR PART?

3. HOW DOES THIS CHAPTER AFFECT YOUR PERCEPTION OF THE CHURCH? HOW WILL IT AFFECT YOUR LEVEL OF PARTICIPATION IN THE CHURCH?

4. WHAT IS AN "EVERYONE CHURCH"?

5. WHAT IS THE KEY MINDSET SHIFT THAT ALLOWS US TO RECEIVE EVERYTHING GOD WANTS US TO EXPERIENCE THROUGH THE CHURCH? WHAT MAKES THIS DIFFICULT?

CHAPTER

1 WHAT AM I BUILDING MY LIFE ON?

2 HOW CAN I HAVE A RELATIONSHIP WITH GOD?

3 HOW DO I CHANGE AND BEGIN MY NEW LIFE IN CHRIST?

4 WHAT DOES GOD WANT FROM ME?

5 HOW DO I HEAR FROM GOD?

6 HOW CAN I EXPERIENCE GOD'S PRESENCE EVERY DAY?

7 WHERE HAS GOD PLACED ME?

8 HOW DOES GOD THINK ABOUT MONEY?

9 WHY IS THE CHURCH IMPORTANT?

10 WHAT DO I DO NOW?

CHAPTER 10

What Do I Do Now?

DISCIPLESHIP & SPIRITUAL MATURITY

WRITE MATTHEW 28:19-20.

WRITE 1 CORINTHIANS 11:1.

In a significant conversation, the defining moment is often known as the "last word." It's the final say. It's the conclusion, the decision, the agreement that determines how you move forward.

When it comes to the goal of the Christian life, there are almost as many opinions as followers of Christ. Depending on who you ask, some might say that it is "to be a good person," "to go to church," "to live a good life," or perhaps "to obey God so you can spend eternity in heaven."

WHAT IF WE GAVE JESUS THE LAST WORD?

Matthew 28:19-20 makes up the last words of the Gospel of Matthew. They're commonly referred to as the "Great Commission." It's not the "Great Suggestion." Jesus expects us to take this seriously. Before He ascended to heaven, Jesus gathered His followers one last time and gave them their marching orders.

He told them to go and make disciples. In order to catch the significance, let's clarify a few things about this profound sentence.

First, the verb tense of "go" is perhaps closer to "as you're going." It's not a one-time trip. It's not "go and make a disciple one time and you're done."

WHEREVER YOU GO, MAKE DISCIPLES.

Second, the reason you have to make disciples is because they don't make themselves.

No one becomes a disciple by accident. It requires intentionality. This begs the question:

WHAT IS A DISCIPLE?

Most people think of a disciple as a spiritual student. You become one by adhering to strict rules and gaining spiritual information.

A DISCIPLE IS MORE THAN A STUDENT; A DISCIPLE IS AN APPRENTICE.

They don't just learn information from a teacher. They follow a master and learn to do what they do. It's more about who you become than what you know.

This is so important to Jesus that He says, "Go to all the nations, tell them to do everything I told you, and I'll be with you in the process all the way to the very end." It's truly a "co-mission." He wants us to do it with Him.

There's no distinction in either **Matthew 28:19-20** or **1 Corinthians 11:1**. This isn't something for a few elite, super-spiritual, professional Christians. It's for everyone.

Although in our culture "Christian" is the far more common term, the New Testament uses the word "Christian" only three times. It uses the word "disciple" more than 250 times.

Jesus told His followers in **Luke 9:23** that if they wanted to be His disciples, they would have to deny themselves on a daily basis. He didn't mean your life would be miserable—He meant you were never intended to be the center of your world. This was the expectation of what it meant to have a relationship with Jesus. The idea of a casual, what's-in-it-for-me relationship with God was foreign to their world.

The apostle Paul gives us a clear, simple definition for discipleship in **1 Corinthians 11:1.**

DISCIPLESHIP IS ONE
CHRIST-FOLLOWER HELPING
ANOTHER CHRIST-FOLLOWER
TAKE THEIR NEXT STEP.
IT'S THAT SIMPLE.

READ 2 TIMOTHY 2:1–6 AND ANSWER THE FOLLOWING QUESTIONS:

1.

What does Paul call Timothy in ***verse 1***?

2.

What does Paul tell Timothy to do in ***verse 1***?

3.

How does Timothy know what to tell people?
(verse 2)

4.

Who does Paul tell Timothy to choose?
(verse 2)

5.

What three occupations does Paul use to compare this process of discipleship?
(verses 3-6)

FOR ANSWERS TURN TO PAGES 154-155

Paul gave Timothy the same blueprint Jesus gave His disciples. The goal of the Christian faith is to make disciples who make disciples. The game plan hasn't changed. The strategy is still the same.

The great news is that you can start doing this today.

It's not about how much of the Bible you know. It doesn't require a family heritage of Christian faith. All you need is a willingness to keep taking steps in your own walk with Christ as well as a desire to help someone else.

This is why Paul stresses strength in the grace of God, reliability, and faithfulness as key ingredients in the process.

You keep showing up.
When you slip, you get back up.
You continue to trust God.
THIS IS THE HEART OF DISCIPLESHIP.

The most common question at this point may be the most basic: Where do I find a disciple? If you're a parent, this is easy. They're in your house. The most important disciples you'll ever lead are in your home. Your children, especially as they get older, follow your example far more than they follow your rules.

But this is an excellent window into discipleship in general. Paul called Timothy his son in the faith. It also gives us a picture of how this works if you don't have kids. The same principle applies in your workplace, with your friends, or anywhere else you go.

THE HARDEST STEP IS CHOOSING TO GET IN THE GAME. WHEN A PERSON DECIDES THEY'RE GOING TO TAKE THIS STEP, GOD BRINGS PEOPLE INTO THEIR LIFE.

The best way to make disciples is to find people with a willingness to grow and then add value to them. As you love and serve them, you build influence. This influence creates trust with the person and a responsibility before God.

This is what makes discipleship different from other forms of authority or leadership. In a discipleship relationship, we don't draw the person to ourselves—we lead them deeper in their relationship with Jesus.

You can't do this simply by adding more information. You have to be able to actually live it. You have to keep growing and taking steps yourself. You never outgrow it. Discipleship isn't a class or a program—it's a person we follow.

BOTTOM LINE: BE A DISCIPLE—AND MAKE DISCIPLES.

REFLECT//DISCUSS

1. HAVE YOU EVER THOUGHT OF THE GREAT COMMISSION AS YOUR PERSONAL MISSION BEFORE? HOW DOES THAT CHANGE HOW YOU GO ABOUT YOUR DAILY ROUTINE?

2. BEFORE READING THIS CHAPTER, HOW WOULD YOU HAVE DEFINED "DISCIPLESHIP"? HOW WOULD YOU DEFINE IT NOW?

3. LOOK AT 2 TIMOTHY 2:3-6 AGAIN. WHY WOULD PAUL COMPARE MAKING DISCIPLES WITH THESE OCCUPATIONS (SOLDIER, ATHLETE, FARMER)? WHAT CAN WE LEARN FROM THE COMPARISONS?

4. DO YOU FEEL READY TO START MAKING A DISCIPLE? WHY OR WHY NOT?

5. WHO IS SOMEONE YOU KNOW RIGHT NOW THAT YOU COULD BEGIN DISCIPLING? PLAN TO REACH OUT TO THIS PERSON THIS WEEK.

CONGRATULATIONS—YOU FINISHED *THE FOUNDATIONS BOOK*!

Taking your next step with God is no small thing. By completing this book, you have responded to what Jesus said in **Matthew 7** all the way back in chapter 1. As you put these principles into practice, you become a wise builder.

Like any relationship, there is no “arriving” with Jesus. Being in His Kingdom means continually being in His presence, investing in and serving others, and continuing to build on the foundation we have learned about. There is always a next step in His Kingdom, always more that Jesus has for you, and always others we can connect with, serve, and develop.

HOW TO KEEP BUILDING ON YOUR FOUNDATION:

READ YOUR BIBLE CONSISTENTLY.
Set goals, get on a reading plan, and grow your intake of His Word over time.

SPEND TIME IN GOD'S PRESENCE.
Submit your heart to God, and pursue time in prayer, worship, and repentance.

GET PLANTED IN A LOCAL CHURCH.
Relationships with others help grow our faith, give us support in challenging seasons, and offer accountability and wisdom for our lives.

OFFER YOUR GIFTS TO SERVE OTHERS.
We all have a way to use our talents for God's Kingdom. Ask Him to show you!

FIND SOMEONE YOU CAN TAKE THROUGH THIS BOOK.
Offering others what we have found in God is valuable and is discipleship in action. Help someone take their next step with Jesus!

ANSWERS

CHAPTER ONE

PAGES 16–17:

1. "Putting into practice" is obeying what you hear Jesus say.
2. It did not fall, because it had its foundation on the rock.
3. A foolish man who built his house on sand
4. It fell with a great crash.
5. Crowds were amazed; He spoke as one with authority, and not as their teachers of the law.

CHAPTER TWO

PAGE 29:

1. Dead
2. All of us
3. In our nature
4. God makes us alive with Christ.
5. The gift of God

PAGE 35:

1. Sin
2. Us
3. So that in Him we could become the righteousness of God

CHAPTER THREE

PAGE 46:

- Death

PAGE 48:

- Salvation and no regret

PAGE 49:

1. Their sin sent Jesus to the cross.
2. Jesus took on the sin of the entire world (including ours) when He went to the cross.
3. They were cut to the heart (overcome with grief/sorrow).
4. Repent and be baptized in the name of Jesus Christ for the forgiveness of sins.
5. The Holy Spirit

CHAPTER FOUR

PAGE 58:

- Keep His commands

PAGES 60–61:

1. They do what He says.
2. Put them into practice
3. They both did.
4. His house was not shaken.
5. Immediately; in the moment

CHAPTER FIVE

PAGE 75:

1. Perfect and refreshing the soul; trustworthy and makes wise the simple
2. Joy to the heart and light to the eyes
3. More precious than gold, sweeter than honey
4. God's servant is warned; great reward for those who keep His decrees
5. Words of his mouth; meditation of his heart

CHAPTER SIX

PAGE 84:

- You, your children, all who are far off, everyone the Lord calls

PAGES 86–87:

1. Advocate/Helper
2. Helps us and is with us forever
3. The world cannot accept Him because they can't see Him and they don't know Him.
4. He lives with us and He is in us.
5. Teach us all things and remind us of everything He has said.

CHAPTER SEVEN:

PAGES 102–103:

1. Teaching, fellowship, breaking of bread, and prayer
2. They were filled with awe from the many signs and wonders.
3. No, they were focused on others and gave to those in need.
4. Glad and sincere
5. Those who were being saved

CHAPTER EIGHT:

PAGE 115:

- They belong to the Lord.

PAGE 116:

- A root of all kinds of evil.

PAGE 117:

1. No one can serve two masters; God and money
2. He says to not worry about our lives.
3. The birds of the air
4. His Kingdom and His righteousness; all these things will be added to you as well
5. Tomorrow will worry about itself; each day has enough trouble of its own.

PAGE 119:

- A tithe of everything belongs to the Lord and is holy.

PAGE 122:

1. No; a cheerful giver
2. Seed; you plant seed
3. In every way; on every occasion; it will result in thanksgiving to God

CHAPTER NINE

PAGE 132:

1. To equip God's people for the works of service that will build His Church.
2. They are unified in faith and mature in the knowledge of the Son of God.
3. The cunning and craftiness of people in their deceitful scheming
4. In love; we grow to become the mature body of Christ
5. It grows and builds itself up in love.

PAGE 134:

- The manifold wisdom of God is made known to all rulers and authorities in the heavenly realm.

CHAPTER TEN:

PAGES 146–147:

1. His son
2. Be strong in the grace that is in Jesus Christ.
3. Things Paul told him in the presence of many witnesses
4. Reliable people who will be qualified to teach others
5. Soldier; athlete; farmer

FOR MORE RESOURCES
VISIT US ONLINE!

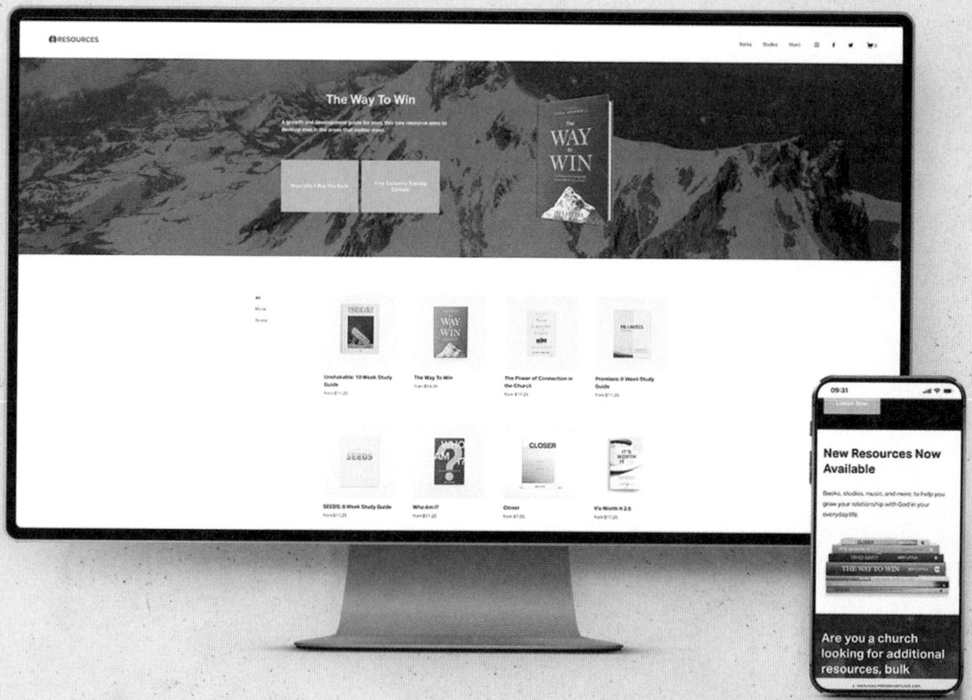

MILESTONERESOURCES.COM